THE STRANGER
on the Road to Emmaus

WORKBOOK

JOHN R. CROSS

D1510636

Published by GOODSEED® International

THE STRANGER ON THE ROAD TO EMMAUS–WORKBOOK
Edition 5

Copyright © 2012 by GOODSEED® International

Email: info@goodseed.com

GOODSEED® International
P.O. Box 3704
Olds, AB T4H 1P5
Canada

ISBN   978-1-890082-78-9

Printed in USA   201209-141-15000

I would like to express appreciation to Meredith DeRidder for pioneering this WorkBook, to my daughter Naomi for taking it the next great leap forward, and to my wife Janice, and my brother David for giving it the final polish.

WHAT THE BIBLE SAYS ABOUT GOD:
Blessed are they who … seek him with all their heart.
PSALM 119:2 NIV

… he who comes to God must believe that He is, and that He is a rewarder of those who diligently seek Him.
HEBREWS 11:6 NKJV

CONTENTS REVIEW QUESTIONS

TAKE TIME TO READ THIS ...

1. This WorkBook is intended to be used with the book entitled, The STRANGER ON THE ROAD TO EMMAUS. THE STRANGER includes approximately 1200 Bible verses quoted with accompanying commentary. Though it's your study guide, it reads like a storybook, not a textbook. If you don't have this book, see the back page of this WorkBook to order a copy. The WorkBook questions and answers are keyed to this book.

2. Learn for the sake of *knowing* for yourself. The point of this book is to study the main theme of the Bible. Whether you believe it or not is up to you. There is no need to argue your present beliefs or future conclusions.

3. Get the big picture first. Don't impede the study's momentum. Unless it is a question needed to clarify subject material being studied, write down your query and save it till the end. Once you have the big picture in mind, you can go back and fill in the details by getting your questions answered.

4. Learn one section at a time, in the sequence it is written. This is not the type of Bible study where you can jump around from one lesson to another. It is important that you read each chapter section in THE STRANGER and answer the questions in this WorkBook first, *before* you move on to the next section. If you answer a question incorrectly, look it up on the page as indicated and briefly review the material. It will only take a minute, but it will help you immensely as you study deeper into the book.

5. If stopping and answering the questions in this WorkBook seems to disrupt the flow of the story in your mind, then set it aside and just read THE STRANGER.

6. Make sure you complete the study. To make a final judgment about the Bible's primary message before finishing the study entails a high risk of drawing wrong conclusions.

7. The questions in this WorkBook should *not* be viewed as an exam or test. They are *review questions* only—to help you make sure you have a grip on the key points. Don't be insulted if you find a question too easy—it means you understand the material. Others may find it difficult. In a number of instances, more than one answer is right. Mark all that are correct. For *fill-in-the-blank* questions, the number of letters in the word are indicated by the line spaces.

8. The content under the label FOR FURTHER CONSIDERATION not only reinforces what you have learned, but helps develop Bible navigation skills.

Now open THE STRANGER ON THE ROAD TO EMMAUS, read the Preface, and then begin with Chapter One. Enjoy your study!

Chapter One
REVIEW QUESTIONS

1 Prologue

There are no questions on this section.

2 Getting Things Straight

1. The Bible has been a best-seller for centuries.
   ❑ True   ❑ False

2. In many ways, the Bible is like a puzzle—to understand it accurately, the pieces must be put together in the right way.
   ❑ True   ❑ False

3. Important keys for gaining an understanding of the Bible are:
   A. learning the simple concepts first, then moving to the more complex.
   B. starting at the beginning and then studying it in the order of events which are said to have happened.
   C. sticking to one theme at a time.
   D. getting the big picture in mind, then if you wish, going back and filling in the details.
   E. All of the above.

4. The Bible addresses many different issues. If you randomly mix these themes or subjects together, the result will be:
   A. a clear understanding of the Bible's message.
   B. an accurate knowledge of Bible basics.
   C. confusion.

5. The stated goal of THE STRANGER ON THE ROAD TO EMMAUS is to (Mark three):
   A. cover key biblical events.
   B. enhance understanding by stringing the Bible's stories together in logical sequence.
   C. give one an extensive and comprehensive understanding of the Bible.
   D. tie the biblical stories together into one continuous and clear message.

3 A UNIQUE BOOK

1. The Bible is unique in the sense that it speaks with harmony and continuity, in spite of the fact that (Mark three):
    A. the authors wrote across a span of 1500 years.
    B. the authors came from different walks of life.
    C. the authors wrote from three different continents.
    D. the authors wrote in 14 different languages.

2. In all, about 40 men recorded _____ books, which, when compiled into one volume, constitute the Bible.
    A. 12   B. 53   C. 66

3. According to the Scripture, who was the author of every book in the Bible?
    A. A single human prophet
    B. God
    C. The Bible does not say

4. God and his words are inseparable, which is one reason the Bible is often referred to as:
    A. God's Word.   B. Scripture.

5. The Bible says that God guided the prophets in such a way that what was recorded was precisely what he wanted written. As necessary, they could add related thoughts.
    ❏ True   ❏ False

6. We have ample reason to be assured that the Bible we have today is _____ what the prophets wrote.
    A. essentially the same as
    B. radically different than
    C. somewhat similar in the essentials to

7. What significant claim does the Bible make about itself in relation to God?
    A. It gives man's ideas about what God is like.
    B. It is God's message to man.

FOR FURTHER CONSIDERATION:

1. In ancient times, a prophet was a messenger who passed on God's words to the people. The message usually addressed aspects of daily living, but almost invariably the prophet's message included things yet to come. This foretelling of

the future had a practical aspect to it. It was a potent test to determine whether a prophet was genuine.

If what a prophet proclaims in the name of the LORD does not take place or come true, that is a message the LORD has not spoken.

DEUTERONOMY 18:22 NIV

A prophet's message was validated by the accurate fulfillment of his prophecies. He had to be 100% correct—there was no room for error.

But a prophet who presumes to speak in my name anything I have not commanded him to say, or a prophet who speaks in the name of other gods, must be put to death. DEUTERONOMY 18:20 NIV

In other words, a prophet had to be 100% right or he was dead. Obviously such a system discouraged "would-be" false prophets.

2. Find the beginning and end of the Old and New Testaments.

3. Identify those parts of the Bible which are *not* God's Word, such as footnotes, Concordance, maps, etc.

4. In a Bible, find and read these verses (BOOK *chapter*:verse): 2 TIMOTHY 3:16; 2 PETER 1:20,21; ISAIAH 40:8

CHAPTER TWO

REVIEW QUESTIONS

1 IN THE BEGINNING GOD...

1. The Bible says that God created himself in eternity past.
   ❏ True   ❏ False

2. The Bible says that God is _____, existing from everlasting past to everlasting future.

3. According to the Bible, what does God need to exist?
   A. The basic essentials of all life
   B. Eternal matter
   C. Nothing

4. God has many names which describe his character. One of these is the name ____ _____, indicative that he is the *self-existent one*.

5. The name LORD focuses our attention on God's position—he is LORD of lords.
   ❏ True   ❏ False

6. As The Most High, God is (Mark two):
  A. seated high in the sky
  B. Supreme Ruler
  C. King of the universe

7. The Bible emphasizes that there is only __ __ __ God.

8. The Bible says God is invisible because he is a __ __ __ __ __ __.

For further consideration:
In a Bible, find and read these verses (Book *chapter*:verse):
  Psalm *102*:12; Psalm *8*:1; Jeremiah *10*:10a

2 Angels, Hosts and Stars

1. The Bible indicates that angels are (Mark two):
  A. innumerable.   B. invisible.   C. equal to God.

2. Angelic beings were created to serve God.
  ❑ True   ❑ False

3. Circle the words that most correctly communicate God's relationship with his created beings.

  He who _____ the paddle, also _____ the paddle.

creates	fixes
buys	owns
breaks	sells

4. When God created Lucifer (Mark two),
  A. he made him perfect in every way.
  B. he was given special responsibilities.
  C. he was no different than other angels.

5. The Bible states that God is worthy of:
  A. no praise.   B. some praise.   C. all praise.

6. The word *worship* means to declare a person's [*wealth* / *worth*].

For further consideration:
In a Bible, find and read these verses (Book *chapter*:verse):
  Nehemiah *9*:6; Psalm *145*:3

CHAPTER THREE
REVIEW QUESTIONS

1 HEAVEN AND EARTH

1. "Genesis," the first book of the Bible, means *beginnings*.
   ❑ True   ❑ False

2. According to Genesis, God created everything we see and don't see. He created (Mark two):
   A. by use of his hands.
   B. simply by speaking.
   C. out of nothing.
   D. using pre-existing materials.

3. The Bible states that God knows and understands everything but is limited in what he can do.
   ❑ True   ❑ False

4. The Bible maintains that only God possesses this triad of attributes. He is:
   A. all - _ _ _ _ _ _ _.
   B. all - _ _ _ _ _ _ _ _.
   C. everywhere present at _ _ _ _ _ _ _ _.

5. The Bible teaches the concept of *pantheism*—that God is *in* everything, and everything is God.
   ❑ True   ❑ False

FOR FURTHER CONSIDERATION:
In a Bible, find and read these verses (Book *chapter*:verse):
   PSALM *139*:1-6;   ISAIAH *40*:25,26,28

2 IT WAS GOOD

1. The Bible says that it took God nine days to create the world.
   ❑ True   ❑ False

2. The Scriptures indicate that the world, as originally created, was different from what we now know.
   ❑ True   ❑ False

3. The whole universe functions according to precise rules, revealing that God is a God of [*chance / order*].

4. Almost instinctively, we treat these natural laws with great respect because we understand that *whenever you have a law, you also have a consequence.*

    ❏ True   ❏ False

5. The Bible says that, "*God saw that it was good.*" In other words, everything He made was:

    A. perfect.   B. flawless.   C. pure.

6. (Use the Word-Bank below to answer the following questions.) God's creation was perfect because perfection is part of his character. Two other words that describe this aspect of the Lord's pure nature are __ __ __ __ __ __ __ __ __ and __ __ __ __ __, both meaning *to be without blemish.*

7. God created the rich variety we see and experience for our enjoyment. God is a God who truly _____ and _____.

    | holy | loves | righteous | cares |

3 MAN AND WOMAN

1. The Bible says that man was created in the image of God. This means that we are exact duplicates of the LORD with all of his attributes.

    ❏ True   ❏ False

2. Which following statement is true?

    A. God breathed life into man.
    B. Man came to life on his own.
    C. An angel gave life to man.

3. Because God was Adam and Eve's Creator, he was also their [*number-one Fan / Owner*]. He knew what was best for them.

4. God commanded Adam and Eve not to:

    A. eat of the tree of life.
    B. eat of the tree of knowledge of good and evil.
    C. eat from any tree in the garden.

5. The ability to [*choose / walk*] is what distinguishes man from a robot. It makes a relationship genuine. It is what gives meaning and depth to the word [*laughter / obedience*].

6. The Bible says that mankind was created to reflect God's grandeur—to honour Him as a son honours his father.

❑ True ❑ False

7. Though Creator of the universe, God was _____ to Adam and Eve.

    A. a close and caring friend
    B. a knowledgeable yet distant instructor
    C. an aloof and indifferent stranger

8. The Scripture teaches us that only perfect people can live in the presence of a perfect God.

❑ True ❑ False

FOR FURTHER CONSIDERATION:

1. In Papua New Guinea, the culture dictates that *he who creates the paddle also owns the paddle*. In a Bible, find and read these verses that illustrate the Creator-Owner connection:

I CHRONICLES 29:11-12; PSALM 24:1,2; PSALM 47:2

2. In the back of many Bibles is a small concordance. This is a tool to help one find a verse. For example, let's say you can remember that God said he would create man in *"his own image,"* but you cannot remember where the verse is found. As an alternative, use an online concordance such as www.biblegateway.com. The advantage of this type of resource is that it allows you to compare and make use of different Bible translations. (Remember that the Bible was not originally written in English.) Try finding the following verse by using either the concordance in the back of your Bible or online by looking up the word *"image"*:

*So God created man in his own **image**, in the **image** of God he created him; male and female he created them. (NIV)*

CHAPTER FOUR
REVIEW QUESTIONS

1 I WILL

1. Lucifer's rebellion was driven by his [*anger* / *pride*], which God hates.

2. The Bible says that because of God's holy nature, he cannot tolerate __ __ __ in his presence.

3. Lucifer became known by other names—names that reveal aspects of his character. Match two meanings with each name. See page 53 if you have trouble.

    A. Devil   a. adversary

                                 b. false accuser

    B. Satan   c. slanderer

                                 d. enemy

2 HAS GOD SAID?

1. The Bible tells us that Satan:

    A. is the great deceiver, the father of lies.

    B. is a harmless jokester.

    C. desires to make us genuinely happy.

    D. is a figment of one's imagination.

2. Satan first twisted God's word to cause Eve to doubt God, then he outright _____ it.

    A. denied   B. ignored   C. approved

3. The Bible says that God considered Adam and Eve's disobedience to be an innocent mistake—a misunderstanding.

    ❑ True   ❑ False

4. A broken law has consequences. The Scripture teaches us that sin's effects are very costly.

    ❑ True   ❑ False

5. Adam and Eve sewed fig leaf clothing for themselves and hid from God because they were experiencing an uncomfortable new feeling called [*guilt / defeat*].

6. Adam and Eve had a __ __ __ __ __ __, to obey or not to obey. God considers all disobedience—even what appears seemingly small—to be __ __ __.

7. Though Adam and Eve's sin hurt their relationship with God, it did not result in any permanent consequences or repercussions.

    ❑ True   ❑ False

8. Adam and Eve made coverings for themselves, but their outward appearance did not remedy the inner reality.

    ❑ True   ❑ False

3 WHERE ARE YOU?

1. The Lord wanted Adam and Eve to sort out in their minds precisely what had happened. *They had disobeyed Him! They had trusted Satan instead of God.*
   ❏ True   ❏ False

2. Adam and Eve (Mark two):
   A. were unwilling to accept responsibility for their sin.
   B. admitted that they had freely followed Satan.
   C. pointed the finger of blame at others for their sin.

3. Adam and Eve's actions affected:
   A. no one but themselves.   B. the whole human race.

4. The Bible also states that Satan would temporarily wound the child, but the child would _____ Satan.
   A. fatally crush   B. seriously injure   C. help

5. The Bible says that a male child was promised to come through the future offspring of Eve. This male child would free mankind from the consequences of sin. He would be known as (Mark all that are true):
   A. the Anointed One.
   B. the Promised Deliverer.
   C. the Chosen One.
   D. the Saviour, or "the one who saves."

6. Because of Adam and Eve's sin, nothing remained perfect. The earth and everything in it suffered from the effects of a:
   A. drought.   B. curse.   C. flood.

7. Just as defying the law of gravity brings broken bones, so violating God's word has ramifications. The most bitter consequence of sin is [*death / failure*].

4 DEATH

1. In the Bible, death implies some sort of separation. It can also mean annihilation or non-existence.
   ❏ True   ❏ False

2. According to the Bible, sin has an inescapable consequence: "The ___ ___ ___ ___ ___ of sin is death..." ROMANS 6:23 NIV

3. Match the following.

___ A. Death of the Body   1. Separation of man's spirit from God

___ B. Death to a Relationship   2. Separation of man's spirit from God forever

___ C. Death to a Future Joy, The Second Death   3. Separation of man's spirit from his body

4. God is holy, therefore He is offended by all sin. He detests and is [*angry against* / *oblivious to*] all sin. He will have no part in it.

5. Speaking of all of mankind, the Bible says man's sins have __ __ __ __ __ __ __ __ __ him from God.

6. God, being perfect, cannot allow sin in his presence. Habakkuk 1:13 NIV says he is *"too pure to look on evil; [he] cannot tolerate wrong."*
   ❑ True   ❑ False

7. The _____ of _____ is a place of unending punishment God created specifically for Satan and his followers.

8. Sinful man will experience the same punishment as Satan. The Bible calls this the _____ death, probably because it occurs after physical death.

CHAPTER FIVE

REVIEW QUESTIONS

1 A PARADOX

1. Just as God established physical laws to govern the universe, so he established spiritual [*suggestions* / *laws*] to govern his relationship with man.

2. The Bible teaches that on the moral ledger, sin incurs a debt that can only be paid by:
   A. being religious.   B. working hard.   C. death.

3. The Bible says *"the soul who sins shall die."* NKJV
   ❑ True   ❑ False

4. Man faces a dilemma that has two facets, like opposite sides of the same coin.
   - We have something we don't want: a [*morality* / *sin*] problem, with all its consequences.
   - We need something we don't have: a [*goodness* / *perfection*] that allows us to live in God's presence.

5. The Bible says that God is just which means that, as a judge, he is fair and impartial.

   ❑ True   ❑ False

6. God revealed a type of love when he created the world, a _____ and _____. But then God unveiled a deeper love, an _____ love. This love is often referred to using the words *grace, mercy, kindness* and *compassion* (Use the best words).

   | concern   undeserved   romantic   care   friendly |

7. God judges [*all / most / the worst*] of our sin, whether here during life on earth, or after physical death.

8. God provided a way for man's sin-debt to be paid in order that man may escape the death penalty. God did this because:

   A. he loved those he created.

   B. Satan demanded it.

   C. man deserves it.

9. The Bible states that the same pride that caused Satan to rebel is what will keep us from coming to God for help. The Lord can only help man escape the penalty of death when:

   A. man humbles himself and seeks God's help.

   B. man is content with who he is.

   C. man finds fulfillment in life.

   D. man helps others.

FOR FURTHER CONSIDERATION:

Using a Bible, find and read these verses: PSALM 96:10; PSALM 98:9; PSALM 101:1. What is their common theme?

2 ATONEMENT

1. Adam and Eve could do nothing, outwardly or inwardly, to [*remove / forget*] the sin problem.

2. The Bible states that __ __ __ __ __ is the consequence of sin.

3. The first of Adam and Eve's children, Cain and Abel, were born sinless.

   ❑ True   ❑ False

4. The Scriptures say, *"Without the* _____, *there is no forgiveness."*

   A. washing with water   NET

   B. shedding of blood

   C. shedding of tears

5. Based on certain future events, God said that he would accept an animal's death in man's place—as man's [*payment / substitute*].

6. The shed blood would provide an atonement-covering by which (Mark three):
   A. God no longer saw man's sin.
   B. God viewed man as now righteous.
   C. Satan would be appeased.
   D. man could now be accepted in God's presence.

7. Cain's offering was not acceptable because:
   A. he did not have confidence in God's instructions as being trustworthy.
   B. he did not come to God in God's way.
   C. he held back on his best garden produce.
   D. his sacrifice could not shed blood.

8. Cain was angry, yet God was gracious and explained to him that if he came the same way his brother had come, he too would be ___ ___ ___ ___ ___ ___ ___ ___.

9. The Bible says that Heaven (Mark three):
   A. is a place for believing men and women.
   B. is an imaginary place.
   C. may or may not exist; we will have to wait to see.
   D. is a place where man's unique relationship with God will be restored.
   E. is a place without pain, tears or death.

3 TWO BY TWO

1. Though the people of Noah's day disregarded the Lord, God _____ their sin. God is grieved by sin.
   A. was unable to do anything about
   B. did not concern himself with
   C. did not overlook

2. Man may have had a life that excluded God, but God still held man accountable for sin.
   ❑ True   ❑ False

3. Noah was different from the other men of his day (Mark two):
   A. because he was a righteous man.
   B. because he trusted God.
   C. because he was a sinner.

4. The Bible indicates that Noah brought an animal sacrifice to God, evidence that he recognized the need to have an innocent substitute pay the [*cultural* / *death*] penalty for him.

5. Man sometimes threatens and never delivers, but God always keeps His Word.
   ❑ True   ❑ False

6. Only an all-powerful God could create the flood circumstances.
   ❑ True   ❑ False

4 BABEL

1. Man wanted to build a tower to bring honour to:
   A. God.   B. the first man, Adam.   C. himself.

2. It is right to exalt ourselves because we are truly deserving.
   ❑ True   ❑ False

3. According to the Scriptures, Babel is the first recorded occurrence of an organized [*rebellion* / *religion*].

4. A definition for the word _ _ _ _ _ _ _ _ is this: *man's efforts to reach God.*

5. The Bible describes mankind as (Mark two):
   A. being in a spiritual wilderness.
   B. lost—unable to find a way back to a right relationship with God.
   C. unable to ever have a friendship with the Lord.

6. In contrast to man's religious efforts, the Bible teaches that the only true way to be made acceptable to God was provided by the Lord himself.
   ❑ True   ❑ False

FOR FURTHER CONSIDERATION:
Find and compare these verses: GENESIS 9:1; GENESIS 11:4

CHAPTER SIX

REVIEW QUESTIONS

1 ABRAHAM

1. Through the promises God gave to Abram, God was telling Abram that one of his descendants would be THE ANOINTED ONE.
   ❑ True   ❑ False

2. Cross out the incorrect answer: God said that because of Abram's [*respect for / confidence in*] God, righteousness was [*credited to / debited from*] Abram's account, offsetting his [*sin-debt / bad luck*].

3. When God looked at Abram, he saw him as _____ because he believed God, offering the blood sacrifice as an atonement-covering for his sin.

    A. happy   B. righteous   C. upset

4. Abram found that to gain *a righteousness equal to God's righteousness* all he had to do was trust the Lord, and God provided it.

    ❑ True   ❑ False

2 Belief

1. Genuine faith is built on:

    A. facts.   B. the way you feel.

2. The meaningfulness of one's faith is determined not by the amount of faith you exercise but rather in whom you are placing your trust and confidence.

    ❑ True   ❑ False

3. Abram's obedience was an attempt to prove to God and to others the genuineness of his faith.

    ❑ True   ❑ False

3 Isaac

1. Abraham had learned that God was utterly trustworthy, so he did just as God requested. He had _____ in God's goodness.

    A. faltering hope   B. absolute faith   C. little belief

2. Though Isaac was Abraham's promised son, Abraham obeyed the Lord because he was convinced that God could choose to raise Isaac from the dead.

    ❑ True   ❑ False

3. Even though God had intervened and told Abraham not to kill Isaac, there still was a death in his place. God provided a _____. It was God's idea.

4. The ram was offered as an acceptable—*or perfect*—sacrifice in Isaac's place. The ram was Isaac's:

    A. friend.   B. pet.   C. substitute.

5. God was giving Abraham another lesson about his character. God tested Abraham by commanding him to take his only son and sacrifice him on an altar to show him:

   A. that He could be appeased through child sacrifice.

   B. that He was an angry God.

   C. truths concerning *judgment, faith* and *deliverance through a substitute.*

6. Match the best parallel sentences below.

   ___ A. Just as Isaac was under God's direct order to *die,*

   ___ B. God did *intervene.*

   ___ C. An innocent *animal* died

   ___ D. Just as Abel had offered a sacrifice to die in *his place,*

   ___ E. Just as God viewed Abel's sacrifice as *acceptable,*

   1. God provided a *substitute.*

   2. so God saw fit to provide a ram as an *acceptable* sacrifice in Isaac's place.

   3. so all mankind is under the sentence of *death.*

   4. so the ram had died in *Isaac's place.*

   5. in *man's* place.

7. This story is a vivid illustration of two people coming to God in God's way, believing that His Word was true.

   ❏ True   ❏ False

CHAPTER SEVEN
REVIEW QUESTIONS

1 ISRAEL AND JUDAH

1. Isaac had two sons, Esau and Jacob. Esau was like Cain—doing his own thing, but Jacob was looked upon as righteous because he came to God by faith,

   A. offering a blood sacrifice as an atonement-covering for his sin.

   B. praying daily.

   C. being a good, hard-working man.

2. God renewed His pledge to Abraham and Isaac through Jacob, saying that through Jacob's offspring would come *The Promised*

   — — — — — — — — — .

2 MOSES

1. Pharaoh enslaved the Israelites because:
    A. they wanted to take control of Egypt.
    B. he needed more laborers.
    C. they were growing too numerous and he feared they might turn against Egypt.

2. 40 years after Moses fled Egypt for murdering an Egyptian, God spoke to him from a flaming bush. As Moses approached the bush, God told Moses to remove his shoes because he was standing on holy ground.
    ❑ True   ❑ False

3. God told Moses that:
    A. he would be justly punished for murder.
    B. he would help the Israelites escape out of Egypt.
    C. he was a gifted man whom he needed.

4. God told Moses to tell the Israelites that it was _____ —the self-existent one—who had sent him to them.
    A. The Almighty God   B. The Most High   C. I AM

3 PHARAOH AND THE PASSOVER

1. God taught both the Israelites and the Egyptians that (Mark two):
    A. he delivers those who trust Him.
    B. he alone is God.
    C. only Israelites could escape God's punishment.

2. God extends grace and mercy to those who come to God in God's ＿ ＿ ＿.

3. Because God is gracious, it was acceptable to skip a few of the commands concerning the Passover as long as one did so with good intentions.
    ❑ True   ❑ False

4. If an Egyptian followed all of God's instructions concerning the Passover because he believed that the Lord was the only true God, then God would also pass over his house.
    ❑ True   ❑ False

5. The firstborn lived, but only because an innocent lamb died. The lamb became the firstborn's substitute.
    ❑ True   ❑ False

6. Match the parallel sentences below having to do with the concept of substitution.

   ___ A. God had accepted Abel   1. the ram died *in Isaac's place.*

   ___ B. When Abraham offered   2. the lamb died *in the place of*
         Isaac as a sacrifice,   *the firstborn.*

   ___ C. With the Passover,   3. because an animal had died
                                       in his place.

CHAPTER EIGHT
REVIEW QUESTIONS

1 BREAD, QUAIL AND WATER

1. The Israelites were content with the Lord's leading.
   ❑ True   ❑ False

2. God told Moses to tell the people to gather only as much bread as they could eat that day. There would be more the next day. God was teaching them that His Word was:

   A. to be trusted when times were good.

   B. true and was to be trusted.

   C. something important for them to consider.

3. Man does not deserve God's loving care, yet God provides for man in spite of his sin. This undeserved love is called *grace*.
   ❑ True   ❑ False

FOR FURTHER CONSIDERATION:

Find and read these verses: NEHEMIAH 9:19-21; ISAIAH 30:18; PSALM 78:38

2 TEN RULES

1. God directed Moses to put a boundary line around the mountain:

   A. to protect man from falling rocks.

   B. to show the Israelites where God lived.

   C. to illustrate the separation that exists between a holy God and sinful man.

2. God told the Israelites that if anything was more important than Him in their lives, then they had broken the first rule.
   ❑ True   ❑ False

3. The Bible says that God does not want man worshipping idols or any other gods because:
   - A. no one knows what He looks like.
   - B. only God is worthy of worship.
   - C. they do not resemble God.

4. Because of who God is, even His name should not be used flippantly or irreverently.
   - ❑ True ❑ False

5. The Bible likens certain types of anger to: _____.

   | murder | temper tantrums | disrespect | stress |

6. God knows our outward actions and what takes place in our:
   - A. hearts. B. minds. C. imagination.

7. Anyone who is deceitful or dishonest is following Satan's agenda because Satan is the father of __ __ __ __.

8. Stealing, cheating and lying are never right.
   - A. True. These are totally contrary to God's character.
   - B. False. Sometimes our well-being or duty requires us to.

9. When God tells man something, one can usually count on it as being true.
   - ❑ True ❑ False

10. Down through the years, God's expectations for mankind have changed dramatically.
    - ❑ True ❑ False

11. The Ten Rules made man aware of what the Lord considered sin.
    - ❑ True ❑ False

3 The Courtroom

1. The Bible says that in order to be accepted by God, man must obey how many of the commandments?
   - A. Any four, completely and perfectly
   - B. The first eight (the last two are discretionary)
   - C. All ten

2. God holds man accountable for all of his sin, even the sin of which he is not aware.
   - ❑ True ❑ False

3. It is possible to obey all ten commands consistently and perfectly.
   - ❑ True ❑ False

4. The Ten Commandments have two main objectives (Mark two):
    A. to silence those who say their lives are good enough to be accepted by God.
    B. to show mankind that we are indeed law-breakers.
    C. to give mankind a list of rules to keep in order that we can be pleasing to God.

5. Just as a mirror exposes the dirt, so the Ten Rules expose man's
    __ __ __.

6. God gave the Law so *that through the commandment sin would become* _____ *sinful."* ROMANS 7:13 NASB
    A. *reasonably*   B. *utterly*   C. *somewhat*

7. The Bible says that all people are sinful from the time of:
    A. birth.   B. conception.   C. their first choice to sin.

8. God directed the Israelites to be *holy*, a word that has to do with God's _____ character.
    A. aloof   B. critical   C. perfect

9. The notion that a person's good living and thinking can outweigh his bad, and therefore merit God's acceptance, is totally foreign to the Bible.
    ❏ True   ❏ False

CHAPTER NINE
REVIEW QUESTIONS

1 TABERNACLE

1. The Israelites were to build a sanctuary. This was (Mark two):
    A. a special place called the Tabernacle.
    B. the same as today's religious sites.
    C. because God needed a house.
    D. an elaborate visual aid created by the Lord.

2. The Sanctuary was divided into two sections: one-third of the structure formed the *Holy of Holies* and the other two-thirds, the *Holy Place*. What separated the two rooms?
    A. A large door
    B. A thick curtain or veil
    C. Eight golden posts

3. Write *HH* beside the furniture found in the *Holy of Holies, HP* beside those items placed inside the *Holy Place*, and *CY* beside those pieces located outside in the *Courtyard*.

   A. _____ The Bronze Altar
   B. _____ The Ark of the Covenant
   C. _____ The Basin
   D. _____ The Lampstand
   E. _____ The Table with the Bread
   F. _____ The Atonement Cover
   G. _____ The Altar of Incense

4. With the Tabernacle completed, the cloud that led the Israelites moved into position over the Holy of Holies, signifying God's presence in the midst of his people.
   ❑ True   ❑ False

5. The [*hand / arm*] on the [*body / head*] symbolized the individual's sin and guilt being moved from the man onto the animal. Because the animal now carried the man's sin, it had to [*suffer / die*]. Death is the penalty for sin. It was a case of the innocent dying in the place of the guilty—as a [*substitute / advocate*].The Bible says that God [*accepted / rejected*] the sacrifice on his behalf.

6. After entering the one and only gate, the first step to approaching God was to offer a sacrifice on the Bronze Altar.
   ❑ True   ❑ False

7. Because death is the penalty for sin, the sacrifice pictured :
   A. what was necessary for sin to be forgiven.
   B. God's need for a blood sacrifice.
   C. Satan being appeased.

8. The Bible says that only the High Priest was allowed to enter the Holy of Holies. He did so only once a year and never without [*food / blood*] which he offered on the Atonement Cover. This was done on the [*Passover / Day of Atonement*].

FOR FURTHER CONSIDERATION:
Find and read the following verse: EXODUS 40:17-38

2 UNBELIEF

1. As the Israelites learned more about the Lord, they also were more _____ for those things they knew.

   | worthy | accountable | esteemed |

2. God may delay judgment on sin for a period of time, but eventually he judges all sin.
   ❑ True   ❑ False

3. God's purpose in judgment is to bring about a change of attitude described by the word *repentance.*
   ❑ True   ❑ False

4. When the Bible uses the word *repent*, it means:
   A. to weep and feel sorry.
   B. to promise to live better.
   C. a change of mind.

5. Only during this life on earth can people repent and be heard by God.
   ❑ True   ❑ False

3 JUDGES, KINGS AND PROPHETS

1. The Bible teaches that because all roads—all beliefs—ultimately lead to the same God, the important thing is simply to trust in God.
   ❑ True   ❑ False

2. Unlike many of the other kings who ruled over Israel, King David trusted God. David called the Lord, "my _____."
   A. Saviour   B. Inspiration

3. Solomon constructed a temple in Jerusalem, possibly on the same site where Abraham was prepared to offer Isaac. It was a permanent structure, similar in design to the portable __ __ __ __ __ __ __ __ __ __ which it replaced.

4. God sent prophets who (Mark two):
   A. warned Israel that the LORD would judge them for their wandering morals.
   B. were popular with the people because they were telling them what they wished to hear.
   C. gave specific information about the coming DELIVERER.

5. While in captivity, the people, who were without a temple, introduced the synagogue as a place for social interaction, teaching and study of the Scriptures.
   ❑ True   ❑ False

6. The _____ were Greek-influenced Jews who took away from God's Word.
   A. Sadducees   B. Pharisees   C. Judges

7. The _____ were strict observers of the Law. They
   were so concerned about keeping the Ten Commandments
   that they created additional rules.

      A. Sadducees   B. Scribes   C. Pharisees

8. Throughout the centuries there were always those people who
   waited in eager anticipation for God to fulfill his promises.
   Most importantly, they were waiting for the arrival of:

      A. Caesar   B. THE PROMISED DELIVERER   C. Pharaoh

FOR FURTHER CONSIDERATION:

Find and read the following verses: ISAIAH 29:13; PROVERBS 1:1-7

CHAPTER TEN

REVIEW QUESTIONS

1 ELIZABETH, MARY AND JOHN

1. The Israelites waited a long time for THE PROMISED DELIVERER
   to arrive. In the verse below, God refers to himself as coming
   to earth and John preparing his way as a messenger. Connect
   the circled words in the verse with the appropriate person or
   group listed below.

       God   John   The Israelites

   *"See, I will send my messenger, who will prepare the
   way before me. Then suddenly the Lord you are seeking
   will come to his temple; the messenger of the covenant,
   whom you desire, will come," says the LORD Almighty.*

                                     MALACHI 3:1NIV

2. The baby was to be called *The Son of God.*
      ❏ True   ❏ False

3. Since Jesus was not born of a human father, he did not have
   Adam's sinful nature. Instead, because God was his father, he
   was perfect, just as God is perfect. He had God's nature.
      ❏ True   ❏ False

FOR FURTHER CONSIDERATION:

In LUKE 1:46-55, Mary is recorded praising the Lord calling him,
"my Saviour." Mary said this, because as a sinner she knew she
needed a Saviour. Read these verses.

2 JESUS

1. Just as God has names that depict his character, so *The Promised Deliverer* was given names that described his character. Match each name with its meaning.

   ___ A. Jesus   1. *God with us*

   ___ B. Immanuel   2. Greek for *Messiah*

   ___ C. Christ   3. *Deliverer* or *Saviour*

   ___ D. Messiah   4. *Anointed One*

2. Over 700 years earlier, the prophet Micah recorded that the *Promised Messiah* (Mark two):

   A. must be born in Bethlehem Ephrathah.

   B. would be born in a royal palace.

   C. had lived *from everlasting.*

3. When the Magi saw Jesus, they bowed down and worshipped him. God's Law was very specific—only _____ was to be worshipped.

   A. the God most High

   B. the current Jewish king

   C. the Roman emperor

4. The name *Son of Man* (Mark two)…

   A. implies Jesus had a human father: Joseph was Jesus' father.

   B. emphasizes Jesus humanity: he took on a human body. He was completely man.

   C. declares Jesus' true identity: for centuries, scholars of Scripture have recognized this name as referring to the ANOINTED ONE.

5. *"In the beginning was the Word … and the Word* _____."

   A. became a god   B. was God   JOHN 1:1 NKJV

FOR FURTHER CONSIDERATION:

1. Find in your Bible the following prophecy and its fulfillment: MICAH 5:2 MATTHEW 2:3-6

2. If your Bible has maps in the back, locate:

Nazareth, Bethlehem, Jordan River, Sea of Galilee

3 AMONG THE SAGES

1. Although Jesus was God himself, he chose to come to the earth as _____.

   | an extra-terrestrial   a human   an avatar |

2. Even as a boy, Jesus made a profound impression upon the scholars in the temple.
   ❑ True   ❑ False

4 BAPTISM

1. Baptism implies:

   | salvation   identification   washing   physical cleanliness |

2. John taught that the Jews had strayed from the Scripture, embracing man's ideas. He said they needed to change their mind about their wandering ways and return to God. Another word for this is _____.
   A. atonement   B. sorrow   C. repentance

3. John identified Jesus as the PROMISED SAVIOUR, the one who would take away the sin of the world. John called him the [*Lamb* / *Gift*] of God and said that Jesus had lived [*with* / *before*] him—eternally.

4. Baptism washes our sin away so we can be acceptable to God.
   ❑ True   ❑ False

5. It is important to recognize that our limited ability to reason cannot fit [*an infinite* / *a finite*] God into our [*infinite* / *finite*] minds.

6. Though it is correct to refer to any person of the Trinity as God, a distinction can be made as follows:

   The Most High = The ___ ___ ___ ___ ___ ___

   Jesus Christ = The ___ ___ ___

   The Spirit = The ___ ___ ___ ___ Spirit

7. The Bible states that God is a tri-unity, or Trinity—the Father, Son and Spirit—but still one God. Using IS and IS NOT, complete the diagram, which assists us in our understanding of the Trinity.

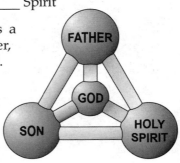

CHAPTER ELEVEN
REVIEW QUESTIONS

1 TEMPTED

1. Although Jesus was God, he was also fully man with real physical needs.
   ❑ True   ❑ False

2. Satan suggested that Jesus turn stones into bread for nourishment. But there was a catch. To do so, Jesus would be:
   A. demonstrating that, as YAHWEH, there was no one greater in the universe.
   B. compromising who he was by following Satan's orders.

3. Jesus countered each of Satan's temptations by quoting:
   A. some respected philosophers.
   B. God's written Word.
   C. his father, Joseph.

4. Jesus responded to Satan's initial challenge by stating that it was more important to be concerned about one's physical needs than to worry about one's spiritual well-being.
   ❑ True   ❑ False

5. Satan loves religion and quoting the Bible is a favorite method of deception. The Devil quoted God's Word accurately and in context when he tempted Jesus.
   ❑ True   ❑ False

6. If Jesus worshipped Satan, he would also be serving him.
   ❑ True   ❑ False

7. The struggle between God and Satan is a balanced battle. Jesus is just as powerful as Satan.
   ❑ True   ❑ False

8. Even those who were closest to Jesus wrote that Jesus:
   A. *committed no sin, nor was deceit found in his mouth.*
   B. *rarely exaggerated or understated when he spoke.*

2 POWER AND FAME

1. Repentance is something that happens inwardly. Jesus intended to begin his rule in the heart.
   ❑ True ❑ False

2. Jesus spoke with authority, but could not demonstrate his claims because he was human.
   ❑ True ❑ False

3. Jesus healed many men and women of physical handicaps and diseases because (Mark three):
   A. he felt compassion for them.
   B. he wanted to establish that he and his message were from Heaven.
   C. he was powerful.
   D. he was trying to gain popularity and influence among the people.

FOR FURTHER CONSIDERATION:

According to the culture of that day, a leper had to shout *"unclean"* whenever anyone approached. It was thought that if a leper was downwind, then you could approach to within 6 feet (2m), but if the leper was upwind, then not even 130 feet (40m) was safe enough. The possibility of physical contact with a leper would not only have been repulsive, but unthinkable.

Yet the Bible says that Jesus reached out his hand and deliberately touched a leper (MARK 1:40-45). That touch was not necessary. Jesus healed many a person from a distance. Think of what that touch meant to the watching crowd—to the leprous man. The event must have been electrifying! Not only was it culturally unacceptable, but according to the Law, if a man physically contacted a leper then he was ceremonially unclean. Not so with Jesus. Rather, there was the opposite effect. Jesus touched the man and the leper became clean. That touch was intentional. It was the touch of God.

3 NICODEMUS

1. When Jesus told Nicodemus that he must be born again, Jesus was referring to a mystical and miraculous rebirth as an infant.
   ❑ True ❑ False

2. The Bible says that Jesus told Nicodemus that if he put his faith in Jesus, he would have __ __ __ __ __ __ __ life.

3. The biblical meaning of the word *believe* should be understood as:
   A. a simple intellectual assent.
   B. a determination to achieve the impossible.
   C. synonymous with faith and trust.
   D. an abstract, mystical acquisition of knowledge.

4. The [*amount / object*] of one's faith is of critical importance.

5. Jesus was promising eternal life, not only to Nicodemus, but to:
   A. those whose good deeds outweighed their bad.
   B. whomever is religious enough.
   C. everyone who believes in him.

6. The Bible states that man is under judgment and destined for eternal death in the Lake of Fire until he puts his trust in Jesus to deliver him.
   ❑ True   ❑ False

7. Jesus declared that there was a middle ground—a "gray zone"—between believing him and being an unbeliever.
   ❑ True   ❑ False

8. The Bible says that you must wait until death to find out your eternal destiny.
   ❑ True   ❑ False

4 REJECTION

1. The Bible says, *"When Jesus saw their _____, he said to the paralytic, 'Son your sins are forgiven.' "* NET

energy   faith   work   love

2. Jesus showed the teachers of the law that he was God by:
   A. forgiving sin.
   B. knowing their thoughts.
   C. healing a paralyzed man.

3. Jesus could only help those who recognized their:

helplessness   heritage   sinfulness   self-worth

4. The religious leaders rejected Jesus as THE PROMISED DELIVERER:
   A. because he worked on the Sabbath.
   B. because he wasn't recognized as a medical expert.
   C. because he gave no consideration to what others thought.

5. All the disciples (apostles) were educated, religious leaders.
   ❑ True   ❑ False

FOR FURTHER CONSIDERATION:
Find and read the following verse: MATTHEW 22:15-22

5 THE BREAD OF LIFE

1. Jesus could see that the people only wanted him to be king so that they could get free food. Jesus (Mark two):
   A. was seeking to rule people's hearts.
   B. said that the people's goal in life should be to pursue that which would give them eternal life.
   C. immediately did another miracle to confirm his deity.

2. When the people asked Jesus what sort of work they would have to do to earn everlasting life, Jesus replied, *"This is the deed God requires—to _____ the one whom he sent."* JOHN 6:29 NET
   A. *make king*   B. *believe in*   C. *serve*

CHAPTER TWELVE
REVIEW QUESTIONS

1 FILTHY RAGS

1. In the parable Jesus told about the Pharisee and the tax collector, the Pharisee was relying on his own right living to make himself righteous before God.
   ❑ True   ❑ False

2. The tax collector was conscious of the fact that he was:
   A. a helpless sinner.
   B. needing to do a multitude of good deeds to be acceptable before God.
   C. a very good and righteous man.

3. God can only work in a heart that is _____.

   | repentant | proud | self-confident | good |

4. Jesus tied repentance to [*humility* / *self-respect*].

5. The Pharisees were relying upon which of the following to become right with God?

    A. Their religious observances   C. Their Jewish birth

    B. Their faith in God's mercy   D. Their good works

6. The Bible is very clear that good works are necessary in order for a person to earn a right standing with God.

    ❏ True   ❏ False

7. The Bible says that all people are:

    A. inherently good.

    B. slaves to sin.

    C. redeemable by good works.

8. God holds everyone accountable for the choices they make.

    ❏ True   ❏ False

2 THE WAY

1. In the Bible passage, JOHN 10:7-10, Jesus likened himself to the _____ of the sheep.

> priest   shepherd   prophet   king

2. Jesus compared those who threaten the sheep to:

    A. those who abuse their animals.

    B. false teachers—those who proclaim another way to God.

    C. those who threaten to assault good people.

3. Just as there was only one way to gain entrance into the sheep pen, the only way to escape the consequences of sin is through belief in __ __ __ __ __.

4. Jesus said: he is the only [*way* / *companion*] to God. His Word is the only [*truth* / *book*]. [*Eternal life* / *Happiness*] can only be found in him.

3 LAZARUS

1. Jesus said that the sickness and death of Lazarus would help the disciples believe.

    ❏ True   ❏ False

2. Martha had faith that Jesus could raise her brother from the dead if he chose to because he was the Messiah.

    ❏ True   ❏ False

3. Though Martha knew Lazarus would be resurrected at the end of the world, Jesus had the power to resurrect him at any moment.

❑ True ❑ False

4. Why did Jesus pray out loud when they rolled the stone away from the tomb?

A. So those listening would believe that Jesus was God.

B. Jesus wanted God to hear him.

C. Jesus wanted the people to know that he was a righteous man.

5. The Bible states that man is destined to die once, and after that to face judgment.

❑ True ❑ False

4 Hell

1. Why did Lazarus go to paradise?

A. He was poor.

B. He had faith and was coming to God in God's way.

C. He had lived a very good life.

2. The rich man went to _____ because he ignored God and lived only for himself. There are no _____ chances in Hell to gain Heaven. _____ can only be received if one _____ and believes during this lifetime.

| second | Hell | repents | Mercy |

3. The Bible says that if man refuses to believe God's written Word, then he will not be convinced even if someone is raised from the dead.

❑ True ❑ False

5 Acceptance and Betrayal

1. When Jesus rode into Jerusalem on a colt, the enthusiastic crowd responded with applause and praise, hoping that he would overthrow their Roman oppressors. They were unaware that in doing so, they were:

A. fulfilling a 500 year-old prophecy given by the Prophet Zechariah.

B. doing exactly what the Pharisees wanted them to do.

2. Because of Jesus' popularity among the huge Passover crowds, the religious leaders were:
   A. planning to kill him publicly as an example.
   B. hoping Jesus would perform another miracle.
   C. afraid to kill Jesus.
   D. wanting to make Jesus king.

3. Jesus said that the Passover loaf represented his [body / friendship].

4. The cup (wine) was symbolic of how Jesus' blood would soon be poured out for many people.
   ❑ True ❑ False

FOR FURTHER CONSIDERATION:
Find and compare the following prophecies and fulfillments:
ZECHARIAH 9:9 ⟶ MARK 11:7-10
PSALMS 41:9 ⟶ MARK 14:17-20
ZECHARIAH 11:12 ⟶ MATTHEW 27:3-7

CHAPTER THIRTEEN
REVIEW QUESTIONS

1 THE ARREST

1. Though Jesus submitted his human will to that of his heavenly Father, he agonized over the suffering he was about to face.
   ❑ True ❑ False

2. When the mob, sent to arrest Jesus, told him who they were looking for, Jesus acknowledged who he was with an emphatic "I AM!" A literal translation of the original language would be:
   A. "I AM in control."
   B. "I AM stronger than this mob."
   C. "I AM, right now, God."

3. In reaction to Jesus identifying himself as "I AM,"
   A. the crowd jeered.
   B. Judas Iscariot scoffed.
   C. the crowd fell backward to the ground.

4. When Jesus told Peter to protect him, he cut off a servant's ear.
   ❑ True ❑ False

5. When the high priest asked Jesus, "Are you THE PROMISED DELIVERER?" Jesus answered, ["I am" / "I am not"].

6. Though a King, Jesus had no political ambitions. His reign began in the hearts of people.
   ❑ True   ❑ False

7. The night court held by the Sanhedrin was legal.
   ❑ True   ❑ False

2 THE CRUCIFIXION

1. The Sanhedrin found Jesus guilty on two charges but only one was accurate:
   A. he claimed to be Christ / Messiah.
   B. he forbid payment of taxes to Caesar.

2. Neither Herod nor Pilate could find Jesus guilty of anything deserving the death penalty.
   ❑ True   ❑ False

3. Crucifixion was a Roman form of capital punishment used only for slaves and criminals of the lowest order.
   ❑ True   ❑ False

4. King David wrote about the Messiah's crucifixion _____ before it became Rome's official form of capital punishment.

200 years	800 years	50 years

5. Jesus assured the thief on the cross next to him that he would go to Paradise, because he was putting his [*wish* / *trust*] in Jesus to deliver him from the consequences of sin.

6. When Jesus died, the Temple curtain which was in front of the Holy of Holies was torn from top to bottom. This was significant because (Mark two):
   A. to look behind the curtain was to die.
   B. the high priest had said such an event would happen.
   C. only God could have torn the curtain. It was impossible for man to have done so.

7. The Greek word which is translated, *"It is finished,"* had many different usages during the time of Christ. Which of the following accurately expresses its meaning (Mark three)?
   A. The job you gave me is finished.
   B. The debt is finished.
   C. My life is done.
   D. The search for an acceptable sacrifice is finished.

8. The day Jesus died was the climax of the Passover week—the day when the lamb was killed.
   ❑ True ❑ False

9. All of this happened on the Day of _____ when the Passover lamb was killed.

Preparation	Atonement	Pentecost

3 THE BURIAL AND RESURRECTION

1. The tomb was very secure because (Mark two):
   A. the disciples spent the night in front of the tomb.
   B. it was guarded by well-trained soldiers.
   C. the entrance to the tomb was sealed.

2. When the angel of the Lord appeared in front of the tomb, the guards initially:
   A. fought the angel.
   B. passed out—overcome with fear.
   C. ran away in terror.

3. The angel told Mary and Salome that Jesus was:

dead	sleeping	risen	in a coma

4. The Bible says that when John saw the empty tomb he:

fled in panic	believed	wept in disbelief

5. Jesus, THE ANOINTED ONE, had crushed Satan's [head / heel], just as God had promised back in the Garden of Eden.

6. Death is the result of sin. Jesus did not have to die, because he was sinless. He died willingly.
   ❑ True ❑ False

FOR FURTHER CONSIDERATION:

Discover how accurate Jesus was in forecasting the details surrounding his death and resurrection:

MATTHEW 16:21; 17:22; 20:18,19

CHAPTER FOURTEEN
REVIEW QUESTIONS

1 THE STRANGER

1. Jesus explained to the two men that Christ had to _____ (Mark three).

> suffer   die   resurrect   reincarnate

2. Jesus used _____ to explain all the events surrounding his death, burial and resurrection.

     A. the Jewish Scriptures   B. a parable   C. history books

2 THE EMMAUS ROAD MESSAGE
— ADAM TO NOAH —

1. Match the phrases below.

___ A. Man *chose his own path*, leading him into a spiritual wilderness.

___ B. Man's *friendship* with God no longer exists.

___ C. Satan *exploits* man to do his will.

___ D. Man joined Satan in *rebellion* against God.

___ E. Sinful man is *separated relationally* from a holy God; at death, man's spirit will be *separated from his body*, and live *forever separated* from God and all future joy.

___ F. Man stands in God's courtroom, *accused* of breaking his holy law.

1. Man is *guilty*.

2. Man is *dead*.

3. Man is an *enemy* of God.

4. Man is *estranged*.

5. Man is a *slave*.

6. Man is *lost*.

2. According to the Bible, man faces three types of death.

___ A. Death of the body: 1. God separated from man.

___ B. Death of a relationship: 2. the spirit separated from the body.

___ C. The Second Death: 3. separated forever from God and all future joy by being confined forever in the Lake of Fire.

3. God created man [*with a will* / *without emotions*] so that by his obedient choices, he would honour God.

4. Man cannot make himself acceptable to God.

    ❏ True   ❏ False

5. Match the following to form complete sentences.

    ___ A. Just as an animal died to clothe Adam and Eve in *acceptable* clothing,

    ___ B. Just as Abel brought a *blood sacrifice* to gain forgiveness for sin,

    ___ C. Just as there was only *one* ark and *only* one door to safety,

    ___ D. Man cannot *reach* or please God through any religious effort,

    ___ E. Just as the people of Noah's day were *judged* for their sins,

1. so God will *judge* all men, regardless of their philosophy of life.

2. so Jesus died to make us *acceptable* in the presence of God.

3. but God *reached* down to man in the person of Jesus Christ.

4. so Jesus is the *only* way to eternal life.

5. so Jesus became the ultimate *blood sacrifice*, dying so that our sin might be forgiven.

6. Man had to die for his sin. But God also loved man, so in his [*mercy / leniency*], he showed man [*tolerance / grace*]. He provided [*work / a way*] for man to escape that death.

7. Although we were born into this world as enemies of God, because of what Jesus did on the cross we can now be friends.

    ❏ True   ❏ False

3 THE EMMAUS ROAD MESSAGE
— ABRAHAM TO THE LAW —

1. Match the following to make complete sentences.

    ___ A. Just as Isaac was bound and could not save himself,

    ___ B. Just as the ram died in Isaac's place,

    ___ C. Just as Abraham's sin-debt was paid when he trusted God,

1. so Jesus pays our *sin-debt* as we put our trust in him.

2. so Jesus died in our *place* and took our punishment on the cross. He is our substitute.

3. so we are bound by sin and helpless to *save* ourselves from its consequences.

2. God credited righteousness to Abraham's *Certificate of Debt* because he was looking ahead to what Jesus would do on the cross.

    ❏ True   ❏ False

3. Jesus died in our place and took our punishment for sin. He is our [*substitute* / *equal*].

4. Which statements are true in relation to the word *believe*?

    A. It is synonymous with trust, confidence and faith.

    B. It is built on fact.

    C. It involves mental assent and heart trust.

5. Jesus cried, *"It is finished,"* because he had done his part in paying our sin-debt. Now we need to do our part.

    ❑ True   ❑ False

6. Match the comparisons between the Passover and Jesus:

    ____ A. The Passover lamb had to be *perfect*.

    ____ B. The lamb had to be a *male*.

    ____ C. The lamb died in the *place* of the first born.

    ____ D. The Israelites were not to break any *bones* of the Passover lamb.

    ____ E. When the angel of death came, he would *pass over* the house that had the blood applied.

    1. None of Jesus' *bones* were broken.

    2. Jesus was *sinless*.

    3. God provided a way for his judgment on sin to *pass over* us. Instead the judgment came to rest on Jesus on the cross.

    4. Jesus died in our *place*, as our substitute.

    5. Jesus was a *man*.

7. Jesus, the *Lamb of God*, was crucified on the same day the *Passover lamb* was killed. He died at the hour the evening sacrifice was offered in the Temple.

    ❑ True   ❑ False

8. Keeping the Ten Commandments helps us restore the broken relationship with God.

    ❑ True   ❑ False

9. Jesus had no sin of his own to die for, so he was able to die for the sins of the whole world.

    ❑ True   ❑ False

10. God says we are *justified*. We are [*sinless* / *declared righteous*].

11. When we are clothed in the righteousness of Christ, in God's eyes we have a *righteousness that is equal to God's holiness.*

    ❑ True   ❑ False

12. We can only be *found righteous* by God if we put our _____ in the fact that Jesus died on the cross in our place.

    faith   trust   confidence   belief

4 THE LAW AND THE PROPHETS
— THE TABERNACLE TO THE BRAZEN SERPENT —

1. We are estranged from God because of our sin.
   ❏ True   ❏ False

2. The animal sacrifice was a temporary payment for sin, but Jesus was the permanent and final Lamb.
   ❏ True   ❏ False

3. The Bible says that man is adopted into God's family with the full rights of a son. Instead of being estranged, man is a son.
   ❏ True   ❏ False

4. Match the following comparison of the Bronze Altar in the Tabernacle courtyard and Jesus.

   The sacrifice was to be ...

   ___ A. from the *herd* or *flock*.

   ___ B. a *male*.

   ___ C. without *defect*.

   ___ D. accepted in man's *place*.

   ___ E. an *atonement-covering* for mans sin.

   ___ F. a *blood sacrifice*.

   Jesus ...

   1. is *sinless*.
   2. died in our *place*.
   3. is the *Lamb* of God.
   4. is a *male*.
   5. was the *blood sacrifice* made for us.
   6. is our way to have *forgiveness* of sin.

5. Match the following to make complete sentences.

   ___ A. Just as the Bronze Altar was the *first step* to God through the blood sacrifice,

   ___ B. Just as the Israelite who brought an animal sacrifice was showing *faith* in God's instructions,

   ___ C. Just as the Tabernacle curtain separating man from God was torn in half, giving man *entrance* into the Holy of Holies,

   ___ D. Just as the only way for the Israelites to be healed from their snake bites was to simply *turn and look* at the bronze serpent,

   1. so Jesus, our substitute Lamb, is the *first* and *only step* to having a right relationship with God.

   2. so God sent Jesus to suffer as a sacrifice for man so that we might *enter* boldly into God's presence.

   3. so we must put our *trust* in what Jesus did on the cross.

   4. so the only way we can become right with God is to repent by simply *turning and looking* in faith to Jesus, believing that he paid our sin-debt.

6. Match the following Tabernacle furniture with the verse that compares Jesus to that object.

___ A. *"I am the way and the truth and the life. No one comes to the Father except through me."* JOHN 14:6 NIV

1. The Lampstand

___ B. *"I am the light of the world. Whoever follows me will never walk in darkness, but will have the light of life."* JOHN 8:12 NIV

2. The Table of Bread

___ C. *"I tell you the truth, he who believes has everlasting life. I am the bread of life."* JOHN 6:47,48 NIV

3. The Atonement-Cover

___ D. *"Their sins and lawless acts I will remember no more." And where these have been forgiven, there is no longer any sacrifice for sin.* HEBREWS 10:17-18 NIV

4. The one Gate

7. Just as Jesus rose from the grave, conquering death, so we become spiritually alive, now and for all eternity.

❏ True ❏ False

8. Although man was once spiritually dead and facing eternal death in the Lake of Fire, those who believe are now spiritually alive and will dwell forever in __ __ __ __ __ __.

5 THE LAW AND THE PROPHETS
— JOHN THE BAPTIST TO THE RESURRECTION —

1. The resurrection showed that Jesus had victory over __ __ __ __ __; he had removed its terrible finality.

2. Match the following phrases to make complete sentences.

___ A. Just as a shepherd searches for and rescues his lost sheep,

1. so we are slaves to Satan and helpless to save ourselves.

___ B. Just as a slave was chained, helpless to deliver himself,

2. so we cannot reach God through good works or deeds.

___ C. Just as there was only one door to a sheep pen,

3. so Jesus left Heaven and died on the cross for us, in our place, to pay our sin-debt in order to rescue us from death.

___ D. Just as the Pharisees could not reach God through keeping the Ten Commandments,

4. so there is only one way to God.

3. Who is responsible for the death of Jesus on the cross?
    A. The Jewish nation alone
    B. The Roman soldiers alone
    C. Every person who has or will ever live

4. On the cross there was a great exchange. Jesus took our _____ and gave us his _____.

    | faith   sin   confidence   righteousness   love |

5. The Bible clearly states that eternal life is a:
    A. gift (something undeserved, free).
    B. reward (something merited).
    C. wage (something earned).

6. It is not the size of our faith, but in [whom / what] we are placing our faith that is significant.

7. By _ _ _ _ _,

    we believe that Jesus died in our place for our sin.

    we believe that Jesus paid our sin-debt.

    we believe that God's justice was satisfied by Jesus' death.

    we believe that God gives us the gift of eternal life.

8. Circle the reasons why Jesus died.
    A. Our sin demanded death.
    B. Jesus had to die for his own sin.
    C. Jesus took the eternal consequences of our sin upon himself.

CHAPTER FIFTEEN
REVIEW QUESTIONS

1 WHAT DO YOU WANT ME TO DO?

1. The Bible says Jesus is coming a second time. We can be sure that this will happen because God always keeps his promises.
    ❑ True   ❑ False

2. The Bible says that if we reject the message of the cross:
    A. we can find other ways to God.
    B. it's guaranteed that we will have other opportunities to accept God's message.
    C. the rest of Scripture will not be understood correctly.

3. The Bible says that you are a sinner; you have a sin-debt that you must forever pay—a debt that requires separation from God in the Lake of Fire. It also says if you believe Jesus paid your sin-debt and trust in Him alone to deliver you from sin's penalty, then God forgives your sin, and your relationship is restored.

   ❏ True   ❏ False

4. If you have put your trust in Jesus Christ, the Bible says that your *Certificate of Debt* was nailed to the cross 2000 years ago, removing your sin-debt.

   ❏ True   ❏ False

5. God forgives us—assuming we will live sin-free lives.

   ❏ True   ❏ False

6. A believer relates to God as a son relates to his father. Their [*fellowship / relationship*] is fixed. They will always be father and son. However, if the son disobeys, then his [*fellowship / relationship*] with his father is broken until he admits his guilt and asks forgiveness.

7. Connect the following icons through the cross.

A. DEBTOR

B. GUILTY

C. ETERNAL JUDGEMENT

D. SLAVE

E. STRANGER

F. ENEMY

G. LOST

1. FOUND

2. SET-FREE REDEEMED

3. RECONCILED

4. ADOPTED

5. DECLARED RIGHTEOUS

6. ETERNAL LIFE

7. CANCELED DEBT

8. The Scripture says that the life a person lives is determined by the [*goodness / focus*] he maintains.

9. What are the things we are to focus on (Mark three)?
    A. What we now have because of Jesus
    B. Getting better acquainted with Jesus
    C. Trusting him with everything
    D. Ourselves and our well-being

10. Which of the following are considered obstacles—things that destroy our focus?
    A. Our human nature—preoccupation with self
    B. The world system—sinful influences that surround us
    C. The Devil
    D. All three of the above

11. Our human nature has an in-built desire to focus on:
    A. God.   B. others.   C. ourselves.

12. Obsession with _____, its needs and desires, is always harmful. We find true joy when we become caught up in knowing _____ and serving _____.

> others   self   God

13. We grow strong spiritual roots as we keep our __ __ __ __ __.

14. There are several things that would help us grow spiritually by maintaining our focus. Match the following:

    ___ A. God himself
    ___ B. By faith
    ___ C. The Bible
    ___ D. Prayer
    ___ E. Telling others
    ___ F. Music
    ___ G. Other believers
    ___ H. Future hope

    1. Helps encourage us.
    2. The disciples went all over, *sharing* this good news.
    3. We gain spiritual maturity through these friendships.
    4. Some day, Jesus will return.
    5. This is how we *walk* with God.
    6. Simply talking to God.
    7. Indwells us in the person of the *Holy Spirit*.
    8. It is a source of daily strength.

FOR FURTHER CONSIDERATION:

Using a Bible, locate the following verses and identify the words that are synonymous with the idea of focus.

COLOSSIANS 3:1-2; HEBREWS 12:2; HEBREWS 3:1

2 A Convenient Time

1. According to the Bible, God in his grace will tolerate sin for a while, but then in his justice he will judge it—either in this life or after death.

   ❑ True   ❑ False

2. For those who may be tempted to put off making a decision to trust Christ, the Bible reminds us that now is the time to do so. Why?

   A. God is trying to force us against our will.

   B. We never know what the future may hold.

   C. The Bible's message never changes.

ANSWERS FOR
CHAPTER ONE

Find the answers on these pages in the book

1 PROLOGUE

No questions

2 GETTING THINGS STRAIGHT

1. True — page 14
2. True — page 14
3. E — pages 14-15
4. C — page 16
5. A, B, D. In such a short book, it is not possible to give one an extensive, comprehensive understanding of the Bible. — pages 14-15

3 A UNIQUE BOOK

1. A, B, C — page 16
2. C — page 16
3. B — page 17
4. A, B — page 17
5. False. It is true that God guided the prophets—that what was recorded was precisely what he wanted written—but these men were not free to add their own private thoughts. — page 18
6. A — page 19
7. B — page 19

ANSWERS FOR
CHAPTER TWO

1 IN THE BEGINNING GOD ...

1. False. The Bible says God had no beginning and will have no end—he is eternal. — page 21
2. everlasting or eternal — page 21
3. C — page 24
4. *I AM* — page 24
5. True — page 24
6. B, C — pages 24-25
7. one — page 25
8. spirit — page 25

2 ANGELS, HOSTS, AND STARS

1.	A, B	pages 26-27
2.	True	page 27
3.	creates, owns	page 27
4.	A, B	page 28
5.	C	page 29
6.	worth	page 28

ANSWERS FOR
CHAPTER THREE

1 HEAVEN AND EARTH

1.	True	page 31
2.	B, C	page 31
3.	False. God knows everything.	page 31
4.	A. knowing B. powerful C. one time	page 32
5.	False. The Bible clearly teaches that God is greater than and separate from his creation.	page 34

2 IT WAS GOOD

1.	False. God created everything in six days.	page 35
2.	True	page 36
3.	order	page 37
4.	True	page 38
5.	A, B, C	pages 39-40
6.	righteous, holy	page 40
7.	cares, loves	page 40

3 MAN AND WOMAN

1.	False	page 41
2.	A	page 42
3.	Owner	page 44
4.	B	page 45
5.	choose, obey	page 45
6.	True	page 46
7.	A	pages 46-47
8.	True	page 46

FOR FURTHER CONSIDERATION:

The concordance should lead you to Genesis 1:27.

ANSWERS FOR
CHAPTER FOUR

1 I WILL

1.	pride	page 52
2.	sin	page 52
3.	A: b, c B: a, d	page 53

2 HAS GOD SAID

1.	A	page 54
2.	A	page 56
3.	False. God considers all disobedience to be sin.	page 57
4.	True	page 58
5.	guilt	page 58
6.	choice; sin	page 59
7.	False. God is holy and therefore cannot tolerate sin in his presence. Adam and Eve's disobedience opened a vast gulf in the relationship between God and man.	page 59
8.	True	page 59

3 WHERE ARE YOU?

1.	True	page 61
2.	A, C	page 61
3.	B	page 62
4.	A	page 62
5.	A, B, C, D	page 63
6.	B	page 63
7.	death	page 63

4 DEATH

1.	False	page 64
2.	Wages	page 64
3.	A: 3 B: 1 C: 2	pages 64-67
4.	angry against	page 66
5.	separated	page 65
6.	True	page 67
7.	Lake of Fire	page 68
8.	second	page 68

ANSWERS FOR
CHAPTER FIVE

1 A PARADOX

1.	laws	page 73
2.	C	page 73
3.	True	page 73
4.	sin, perfection	page 74
5.	True	page 74
6.	care and concern; undeserved	page 75
7.	all	page 75
8.	A	page 76
9.	A	page 76

2 ATONEMENT

1.	remove	page 76
2.	death	page 77
3.	False. Cain and Abel inherited Adam's sin nature.	page 77
4.	B	page 78
5.	substitute	page 78
6.	A, B, D	page 78
7.	A, B, D	pages 79-80
8.	accepted	page 81
9.	A, D, E	page 83

3 TWO BY TWO

1.	C	page 86
2.	True	page 87
3.	A, B	page 87
4.	death	page 87
5.	True	page 89
6.	True	page 90

4 BABEL

1.	C	page 94
2.	False	page 94
3.	religion	page 94
4.	religion	page 95
5.	A, B	page 95
6.	True	page 95

ANSWERS FOR
CHAPTER SIX

1 Abraham

1. True	page 100
2. confidence in, credited to, sin-debt	pages 101-102
3. B	page 102
4. True	page 102

2 Belief

1. A	page 102
2. True	page 103
3. False. Because Abram trusted God, the natural result was that he did the things God wanted him to do.	page 103

3 Isaac

1. B	page 106
2. True	page 106
3. substitute, animal, or ram	pages 108-109
4. C	page 109
5. C	page 109
6. A: 3 B: 1 C: 5 D: 4 E: 2	page 109
7. True	page 109

ANSWERS FOR
CHAPTER SEVEN

1 Israel and Judah

1. A	page 111
2. Deliverer	page 111

2 Moses

1. C	page 112
2. True	pages 113-114
3. B	page 114
4. C	page 114

3 Pharaoh and the Passover

1. A, B	page 116
2. way	page 120
3. False. God gave specific instructions to the Israelites and made it clear that they were to be obeyed.	page 119

4. True	pages 119-120
5. True	page 120
6. A: 3 B: 1 C: 2	page 120

ANSWERS FOR
CHAPTER EIGHT

1 BREAD, QUAIL AND WATER

1. False. They grumbled and complained.	page 123
2. B	page 124
3. True	page 125

2 TEN RULES

1. C	page 127
2. True	page 128
3. B	page 128
4. True	page 129
5. murder	page 130
6. A, B, C	page 130
7. lies	page 131
8. A	page 132
9. False. We can always count on it being true.	page 131
10. False. God's expectations have remained constant and unchanging.	page 132
11. True	page 132

3 THE COURTROOM

1. C	page 133
2. True	page 133
3. False. We are incapable of keeping the law consistently and perfectly.	page 134
4. A, B	page 134
5. sin	page 135
6. B	page 135
7. A	page 135
8. C	page 136
9. True	page 138

ANSWERS FOR
CHAPTER NINE

1 TABERNACLE

1. A, D	page 141
2. B	page 141

3. A: CY   B: HH   C: CY   D: HP
   E: HP   F: HH   G: HP   pages 142-143
4. True   page 144
5. hand, head, die, substitute, accepted   page 146
6. True   page 145
7. A   page 146
8. blood, Day of Atonement   page 147

2 Unbelief

1. accountable   page 148
2. True   page 148
3. True   page 149
4. C   page 149
5. True   page 149

3 Judges, Kings and Prophets

1. False   page 151
2. A   page 151
3. tabernacle   page 152
4. A, C   page 152
5. True   page 153
6. A   page 154
7. C   page 154
8. B   page 155

ANSWERS FOR
CHAPTER TEN

1 Elizabeth, Mary and John

1.   God   John   The Israelites   page 160

"See, I will send my messenger, who will prepare the
way before me. Then suddenly the Lord you are seeking
will come to his temple; the messenger of the covenant,
whom you desire, will come," says the LORD Almighty.

Malachi 3:1

2. True   page 161
3. True   page 161

2 Jesus

1. A: 3   B: 1   C: 2   D: 4   pages 163, 165
2. A, C   page 166
3. A   page 167

3 AMONG THE SAGES

4 BAPTISM

ANSWERS FOR
CHAPTER ELEVEN

1 TEMPTED

2 POWER AND FAME

3 NICODEMUS

1. False. He was referring to a spiritual rebirth.   page 184
2. eternal   page 184
3. C   page 184
4. object   page 184
5. C   page 185
6. True   page 185
7. False   page 185
8. False   page 185

4 REJECTION

1. faith   page 186
2. A, B, C   page 187
3. helplessness, sinfulness   page 188
4. A   page 189
5. False. None of the disciples were religious leaders.   page 189

5 THE BREAD OF LIFE

1. A, B   pages 190-191
2. B   page 191

ANSWERS FOR
CHAPTER TWELVE

1 FILTHY RAGS

1. True   page 193
2. A   page 193
3. repentant   page 193
4. humility   page 193
5. A, C, D   page 194
6. False. The Bible is clear that good deeds cannot earn a right standing with God   page 194
7. B   page 195
8. True   page 195

2 THE WAY

1. shepherd   page 197
2. B   page 196
3. Jesus   page 197
4. way, truth, eternal life   page 197

3 LAZARUS

1. True   page 198

2. True	page 198
3. True	page 198
4. A	page 199
5. True	page 200

4 HELL

1. B	page 201
2. Hell, second, Mercy, repents	pages 201-202
3. True	page 202

5 ACCEPTANCE AND BETRAYAL

1. A	page 203
2. C	page 203
3. body	page 204
4. True	page 205

ANSWERS FOR
CHAPTER THIRTEEN

1 THE ARREST

1. True	page 207
2. C	page 207
3. C	page 208
4. False. It is true that Peter cut off the servant's ear, but Jesus did not tell Peter to protect him.	page 208
5. *I AM*	page 208
6. True	page 211
7. False. Night courts were illegal.	page 210

2 THE CRUCIFIXION

1. A	page 210
2. True	page 213
3. True	page 215
4. 800 years	page 216
5. trust	page 218
6. A, C	page 219
7. A, B, D	page 220
8. True	page 221
9. Preparation	page 220

3 THE BURIAL AND RESURRECTION

1. B, C	pages 222-223
2. B	page 223

3. risen	page 223
4. believed	page 224
5. head	page 226
6. True	page 227

ANSWERS FOR
CHAPTER FOURTEEN

1 The Emmaus Road Message

1. suffer, die, resurrect	page 230
2. A	page 231

2 The Emmaus Road Message
— Adam to Noah —

1. A: 6 B: 4 C: 5 D: 3 E: 2 F: 1	page 232
2. A: 2 B: 1 C: 3	page 232
3. with a will	page 231
4. True	page 233
5. A: 2 B: 5 C: 4 D: 3 E: 1	pages 233-237
6. mercy, grace, a way	page 237
7. True	page 235

3 The Emmaus Road Message
— Abraham to the Law —

1. A: 3 B: 2 C: 1	pages 237-238
2. True	page 238
3. substitute	page 238
4. A, B, C	page 239
5. True	page 238
6. A: 2 B: 5 C: 4 D: 1 E: 3	page 240
7. True	page 241
8. False. The Ten Commands show us that we are sinners who can only come to God in God's way.	page 241
9. True	page 242
10. declared righteous	page 243
11. True	page 243
12. All are correct	page 243

4 The Emmaus Road Message
— The Tabernacle to the Brazen Serpent —

1. True	page 246
2. True	page 247

3. True — page 246
4. A: 3　B: 4　C: 1　D: 2　E: 6　F: 5 — page 245
5. A: 1　B: 3　C: 2　D: 4 — pages 245-248
6. A: 4　B: 1　C: 2　D: 3 — pages 244-247
7. True — page 248
8. Heaven — page 249

5 THE EMMAUS ROAD MESSAGE
— JOHN THE BAPTIST TO THE RESURRECTION —

1. death — page 251
2. A: 3　B: 1　C: 4　D: 2 — pages 249-255
3. C — page 251
4. sin, righteousness — page 250
5. A — page 255
6. whom — page 256
7. faith — page 255
8. A and C — page 257

ANSWERS FOR
CHAPTER FIFTEEN

1 WHAT DO YOU WANT ME TO DO?

1. True — page 259
2. C — page 261
3. True — pages 261-262
4. True — page 262
5. False. If we are trusting in God, his forgiveness is unconditional and total. — page 263
6. relationship, fellowship — page 263
7. A: 7　B: 5　C: 6　D: 2　E: 4　F: 3　G: 1 — pages 264-265
8. focus — page 263
9. A, B, C — page 266
10. D — pages 267-268
11. C — page 267
12. self, God, others — page 268
13. focus — page 268
14. A: 7　B: 5　C: 8　D: 6　E: 2　F: 1　G: 3　H: 4 — pages 269-272

2 A CONVENIENT TIME

1. True — page 274
2. B, C — page 275

GoodSeed® International

P. O. Box 3704

Olds, AB T4H 1P5

CANADA

Business: 403 556-9955

Facsimile: 403 556-9950

Email: info@goodseed.com

GoodSeed Australia
1800 897-333
info.au@goodseed.com

GoodSeed Canada
800 442-7333
info.ca@goodseed.com

BonneSemence Canada
Service en français
888 314-3623
info.qc@goodseed.com

GoodSeed Europe
info.eu@goodseed.com

GoodSeed UK
0800 073-6340
info.uk@goodseed.com

GoodSeed USA
888 654-7333
info.us@goodseed.com

www.goodseed.com

GoodSeed® International is a not-for-profit organization that exists for the purpose of clearly communicating the contents of this book in this language and others. We invite you to contact us if you are interested in ongoing projects or translations.